P9-DCR-709

KNOW YOUR GOVERNMENT

The U.S.
Secret Service

KNOW YOUR GOVERNMENT

The U.S. Secret Service

Gregory Matusky
and
John P. Hayes

CHELSEA HOUSE PUBLISHERS

Editor-in-Chief: Nancy Toff
Executive Editor: Remmel T. Nunn
Managing Editor: Karyn Gullen Browne
Copy Chief: Juliann Barbato
Picture Editor: Adrian G. Allen
Art Director: Giannella Garrett
Manufacturing Manager: Gerald Levine

Staff for THE U.S. SECRET SERVICE

Senior Editor: Kathy Kuhtz
Associate Editor: Pierre Hauser
Copyeditor: Karen Hammonds
Deputy Copy Chief: Ellen Scordato
Editorial Assistant: Theodore Keyes
Picture Research: Dixon & Turner Research Associates
Designer: Noreen M. Lamb
Production Coordinator: Joseph Romano

First Printing

1 3 5 7 9 8 6 4 2

Library of Congress Cataloging-in-Publication Data

Matusky, Gregory.
  The U.S. Secret Service / Gregory Matusky and John P. Hayes.
    p. cm.—(Know your government)
  Bibliography: p.
  Includes index.
  ISBN 1-55546-130-1
  1. United States. Secret Service—Juvenile literature.
I. Hayes. John Phillip. 1949–   II. Title III. Title: United
States Secret Service. IV. Series: Know your government (New York,
N.Y.)   87-30276
HV8141.M27 1988   CIP
363.2'83'0973—dc19   AC

CONTENTS

KNOW YOUR GOVERNMENT

THE AMERICAN RED CROSS

THE BUREAU OF INDIAN AFFAIRS

THE CENTRAL INTELLIGENCE AGENCY

THE COMMISSION ON CIVIL RIGHTS

THE DEPARTMENT OF AGRICULTURE

THE DEPARTMENT OF THE AIR FORCE

THE DEPARTMENT OF THE ARMY

THE DEPARTMENT OF COMMERCE

THE DEPARTMENT OF DEFENSE

THE DEPARTMENT OF EDUCATION

THE DEPARTMENT OF ENERGY

THE DEPARTMENT OF HEALTH AND HUMAN SERVICES

THE DEPARTMENT OF HOUSING AND URBAN DEVELOPMENT

THE DEPARTMENT OF THE INTERIOR

THE DEPARTMENT OF JUSTICE

THE DEPARTMENT OF LABOR

THE DEPARTMENT OF THE NAVY

THE DEPARTMENT OF STATE

THE DEPARTMENT OF TRANSPORTATION

THE DEPARTMENT OF THE TREASURY

THE DRUG ENFORCEMENT ADMINISTRATION

THE ENVIRONMENTAL PROTECTION AGENCY

THE EQUAL EMPLOYMENT OPPORTUNITIES COMMISSION

THE FEDERAL AVIATION ADMINISTRATION

THE FEDERAL BUREAU OF INVESTIGATION

THE FEDERAL COMMUNICATIONS COMMISSION

THE FEDERAL GOVERNMENT: HOW IT WORKS

THE FEDERAL RESERVE SYSTEM

THE FEDERAL TRADE COMMISSION

THE FOOD AND DRUG ADMINISTRATION

THE FOREST SERVICE

THE HOUSE OF REPRESENTATIVES

THE IMMIGRATION AND NATURALIZATION SERVICE

THE INTERNAL REVENUE SERVICE

THE LIBRARY OF CONGRESS

THE NATIONAL AERONAUTICS AND SPACE ADMINISTRATION

THE NATIONAL ARCHIVES AND RECORDS ADMINISTRATION

THE NATIONAL FOUNDATION ON THE ARTS AND HUMANITIES

THE NATIONAL PARK SERVICE

THE NATIONAL SCIENCE FOUNDATION

THE NUCLEAR REGULATORY COMMISSION

THE PEACE CORPS

THE PRESIDENCY

THE PUBLIC HEALTH SERVICE

THE SECURITIES AND EXCHANGE COMMISSION

THE SENATE

THE SMALL BUSINESS ADMINISTRATION

THE SMITHSONIAN

THE SUPREME COURT

THE TENNESSEE VALLEY AUTHORITY

THE U.S. ARMS CONTROL AND DISARMAMENT AGENCY

THE U.S. COAST GUARD

THE U.S. CONSTITUTION

THE U.S. FISH AND WILDLIFE SERVICE

THE U.S. INFORMATION AGENCY

THE U.S. MARINE CORPS

THE U.S. MINT

THE U.S. POSTAL SERVICE

THE U.S. SECRET SERVICE

THE VETERANS ADMINISTRATION

CHELSEA HOUSE PUBLISHERS

INTRODUCTION

Government: Crises of Confidence

Arthur M. Schlesinger, jr.

From the start, Americans have regarded their government with a mixture of reliance and mistrust. The men who founded the republic did not doubt the indispensability of government. "If men were angels," observed the 51st Federalist Paper, "no government would be necessary." But men are not angels. Because human beings are subject to wicked as well as to noble impulses, government was deemed essential to assure freedom and order.

At the same time, the American revolutionaries knew that government could also become a source of injury and oppression. The men who gathered in Philadelphia in 1787 to write the Constitution therefore had two purposes in mind. They wanted to establish a strong central authority and to limit that central authority's capacity to abuse its power.

To prevent the abuse of power, the Founding Fathers wrote two basic principles into the new Constitution. The principle of federalism divided power between the state governments and the central authority. The principle of the separation of powers subdivided the central authority itself into three branches—the executive, the legislative, and the judiciary—so that "each may be a check on the other." The *Know Your Government* series focuses on the major executive departments and agencies in these branches of the federal government.

7

The Constitution did not plan the executive branch in any detail. After vesting the executive power in the president, it assumed the existence of "executive departments" without specifying what these departments should be. Congress began defining their functions in 1789 by creating the Departments of State, Treasury, and War. The secretaries in charge of these departments made up President Washington's first cabinet. Congress also provided for a legal officer, and President Washington soon invited the attorney general, as he was called, to attend cabinet meetings. As need required, Congress created more executive departments.

Setting up the cabinet was only the first step in organizing the American state. With almost no guidance from the Constitution, President Washington, seconded by Alexander Hamilton, his brilliant secretary of the treasury, equipped the infant republic with a working administrative structure. The Federalists believed in both executive energy and executive accountability and set high standards for public appointments. The Jeffersonian opposition had less faith in strong government and preferred local government to the central authority. But when Jefferson himself became president in 1801, although he set out to change the direction of policy, he found no reason to alter the framework the Federalists had erected.

By 1801 there were about 3,000 federal civilian employees in a nation of a little more than 5 million people. Growth in territory and population steadily enlarged national responsibilities. Thirty years later, when Jackson was president, there were more than 11,000 government workers in a nation of 13 million. The federal establishment was increasing at a faster rate than the population.

Jackson's presidency brought significant changes in the federal service. He believed that the executive branch contained too many officials who saw their jobs as "species of property" and as "a means of promoting individual interest." Against the idea of a permanent service based on life tenure, Jackson argued for the periodic redistribution of federal offices, contending that this was the democratic way and that official duties could be made "so plain and simple that men of intelligence may readily qualify themselves for their performance." He called this policy rotation-in-office. His opponents called it the spoils system.

In fact, partisan legend exaggerated the extent of Jackson's removals. More than 80 percent of federal officeholders retained their jobs. Jackson discharged no larger a proportion of government workers than Jefferson had done a generation earlier. But the rise in these years of mass political parties gave federal patronage new importance as a means of building the party and of rewarding activists. Jackson's successors were less restrained in the distribu-

8

tion of spoils. As the federal establishment grew—to nearly 40,000 by 1861—the politicization of the public service excited increasing concern.

After the Civil War the spoils system became a major political issue. High-minded men condemned it as the root of all political evil. The spoilsmen, said the British commentator James Bryce, "have distorted and depraved the mechanism of politics." Patronage, by giving jobs to unqualified, incompetent, and dishonest persons, lowered the standards of public service and nourished corrupt political machines. Office-seekers pursued presidents and cabinet secretaries without mercy. "Patronage," said Ulysses S. Grant after his presidency, "is the bane of the presidential office." "Every time I appoint someone to office," said another political leader, "I make a hundred enemies and one ingrate." George William Curtis, the president of the National Civil Service Reform League, summed up the indictment. He said,

> The theory which perverts public trusts into party spoils, making public
> employment dependent upon personal favor and not on proved merit,
> necessarily ruins the self-respect of public employees, destroys the
> function of party in a republic, prostitutes elections into a desperate
> strife for personal profit, and degrades the national character by lower-
> ing the moral tone and standard of the country.

The object of civil service reform was to promote efficiency and honesty in the public service and to bring about the ethical regeneration of public life. Over bitter opposition from politicians, the reformers in 1883 passed the Pendleton Act, establishing a bipartisan Civil Service Commission, competitive examinations, and appointment on merit. The Pendleton Act also gave the president authority to extend by executive order the number of "classified" jobs—that is, jobs subject to the merit system. The act applied initially only to about 14,000 of the more than 100,000 federal positions. But by the end of the 19th century 40 percent of federal jobs had moved into the classified category.

Civil service reform was in part a response to the growing complexity of American life. As society grew more organized and problems more technical, official duties were no longer so plain and simple that any person of intelligence could perform them. In public service, as in other areas, the all-round man was yielding ground to the expert, the amateur to the professional. The excesses of the spoils system thus provoked the counter-ideal of scientific public administration, separate from politics and, as far as possible, insulated against it.

The cult of the expert, however, had its own excesses. The idea that administration could be divorced from policy was an illusion. And in the realm of policy, the expert, however much segregated from partisan politics, can never attain perfect objectivity. He remains the prisoner of his own set of values. It is these values rather than technical expertise that determine fundamental judgments of public policy. To turn over such judgments to experts, moreover, would be to abandon democracy itself; for in a democracy final decisions must be made by the people and their elected representatives. "The business of the expert," the British political scientist Harold Laski rightly said, "is to be on tap and not on top."

Politics, however, were deeply ingrained in American folkways. This meant intermittent tension between the presidential government, elected every four years by the people, and the permanent government, which saw presidents come and go while it went on forever. Sometimes the permanent government knew better than its political masters; sometimes it opposed or sabotaged valuable new initiatives. In the end a strong president with effective cabinet secretaries could make the permanent government responsive to presidential purpose, but it was often an exasperating struggle.

The struggle within the executive branch was less important, however, than the growing impatience with bureaucracy in society as a whole. The 20th century saw a considerable expansion of the federal establishment. The Great Depression and the New Deal led the national government to take on a variety of new responsibilities. The New Deal extended the federal regulatory apparatus. By 1940, in a nation of 130 million people, the number of federal workers for the first time passed the 1 million mark. The Second World War brought federal civilian employment to 3.8 million in 1945. With peace, the federal establishment declined to around 2 million by 1950. Then growth resumed, reaching 2.8 million by the 1980s.

The New Deal years saw rising criticism of "big government" and "bureaucracy." Businessmen resented federal regulation. Conservatives worried about the impact of paternalistic government on individual self-reliance, on community responsibility, and on economic and personal freedom. The nation in effect renewed the old debate between Hamilton and Jefferson in the early republic, although with an ironic exchange of positions. For the Hamiltonian constituency, the "rich and well-born," once the advocate of affirmative government, now condemned government intervention, while the Jeffersonian constituency, the plain people, once the advocate of a weak central government and of states' rights, now favored government intervention.

In the 1980s, with the presidency of Ronald Reagan, the debate has burst out with unusual intensity. According to conservatives, government intervention abridges liberty, stifles enterprise, and is inefficient, wasteful, and arbitrary. It disturbs the harmony of the self-adjusting market and creates worse troubles than it solves. Get government off our backs, according to the popular cliché, and our problems will solve themselves. When government is necessary, let it be at the local level, close to the people. Above all, stop the inexorable growth of the federal government.

In fact, for all the talk about the "swollen" and "bloated" bureaucracy, the federal establishment has not been growing as inexorably as many Americans seem to believe. In 1949, it consisted of 2.1 million people. Thirty years later, while the country had grown by 70 million, the federal force had grown only by 750,000. Federal workers were a smaller percentage of the population in 1985 than they were in 1955—or in 1940. The federal establishment, in short, has not kept pace with population growth. Moreover, national defense and the postal service account for 60 percent of federal employment.

Why then the widespread idea about the remorseless growth of government? It is partly because in the 1960s the national government assumed new and intrusive functions: affirmative action in civil rights, environmental protection, safety and health in the workplace, community organization, legal aid to the poor. Although this enlargement of the federal regulatory role was accompanied by marked growth in the size of government on all levels, the expansion has taken place primarily in state and local government. Whereas the federal force increased by only 27 percent in the 30 years after 1950, the state and local government force increased by an astonishing 212 percent.

Despite the statistics, the conviction flourishes in some minds that the national government is a steadily growing behemoth swallowing up the liberties of the people. The foes of Washington prefer local government, feeling it is closer to the people and therefore allegedly more responsive to popular needs. Obviously there is a great deal to be said for settling local questions locally. But local government is characteristically the government of the locally powerful. Historically, the way the locally powerless have won their human and constitutional rights has often been through appeal to the national government. The national government has vindicated racial justice against local bigotry, defended the Bill of Rights against local vigilantism, and protected natural resources against local greed. It has civilized industry and secured the rights of labor organizations. Had the states' rights creed prevailed, there would perhaps still be slavery in the United States.

The national authority, far from diminishing the individual, has given most Americans more personal dignity and liberty than ever before. The individual freedoms destroyed by the increase in national authority have been in the main the freedom to deny black Americans their rights as citizens; the freedom to put small children to work in mills and immigrants in sweatshops; the freedom to pay starvation wages, require barbarous working hours, and permit squalid working conditions; the freedom to deceive in the sale of goods and securities; the freedom to pollute the environment—all freedoms that, one supposes, a civilized nation can readily do without.

"Statements are made," said President John F. Kennedy in 1963, "labelling the Federal Government an outsider, an intruder, an adversary. . . . The United States Government is not a stranger or not an enemy. It is the people of fifty states joining in a national effort. . . . Only a great national effort by a great people working together can explore the mysteries of space, harvest the products at the bottom of the ocean, and mobilize the human, natural, and material resources of our lands."

So an old debate continues. However, Americans are of two minds. When pollsters ask large, spacious questions—Do you think government has become too involved in your lives? Do you think government should stop regulating business?—a sizable majority opposes big government. But when asked specific questions about the practical work of government—Do you favor social security? unemployment compensation? Medicare? health and safety standards in factories? environmental protection? government guarantee of jobs for everyone seeking employment? price and wage controls when inflation threatens?—a sizable majority approves of intervention.

In general, Americans do not want less government. What they want is more efficient government. They want government to do a better job. For a time in the 1970s, with Vietnam and Watergate, Americans lost confidence in the national government. In 1964, more than three-quarters of those polled had thought the national government could be trusted to do right most of the time. By 1980 only one-quarter was prepared to offer such trust. But by 1984 trust in the federal government to manage national affairs had climbed back to 45 percent.

Bureaucracy is a term of abuse. But it is impossible to run any large organization, whether public or private, without a bureaucracy's division of labor and hierarchy of authority. And we live in a world of large organizations. Without bureaucracy modern society would collapse. The problem is not to abolish bureaucracy, but to make it flexible, efficient, and capable of innovation.

Two hundred years after the drafting of the Constitution, Americans still regard government with a mixture of reliance and mistrust—a good combination. Mistrust is the best way to keep government reliable. Informed criticism is the means of correcting governmental inefficiency, incompetence, and arbitrariness; that is, of best enabling government to play its essential role. For without government, we cannot attain the goals of the Founding Fathers. Without an understanding of government, we cannot have the informed criticism that makes government do the job right. It is the duty of every American citizen to know our government—which is what this series is all about.

Secret Service agent, automatic weapon drawn, shouts orders to other officers after President Reagan was shot outside the Washington Hilton hotel. Agents are best known as the protectors of the president.

ONE

Protecting the President and the Currency

It seemed a routine day in the life of President Ronald Reagan. The date was March 30, 1981. The president left the White House in the early afternoon and traveled by motorcade a few short blocks to a local hotel. There he gave a speech to 4,000 people. Nothing appeared suspicious. The listeners responded to Reagan's comments and enthusiastically applauded his speech.

Moments later, the president left the stage, walked through the hotel, and headed toward the street. Outside, a small crowd of spectators had gathered. Among them was John W. Hinckley, Jr. With a friendly round face and sandy blond hair, Hinckley seemed a harmless figure. But in reality, the young man suffered from severe mental illness. He was there that day to kill the president.

President Reagan emerged from the hotel. With him walked political advisers and a small group of highly trained personnel known as U.S. Secret Service agents. The crowd applauded the president. He lifted his right arm in response. Television cameras recorded the event.

Suddenly, a loud blast shattered the atmosphere. The crowd scrambled for safety. The men guarding the president realized the noise was gunfire, and they flew into action. Secret Service agent Tim McCarthy jumped in front of the president with his arms and legs spread. A bullet hit him in the stomach.

President Gerald R. Ford (right) rides a ski lift in Vail, Colorado, with a Secret Service agent. Agents protect the president at all times, even when he vacations.

Before the next shot, Secret Service agent Dennis McCarthy spotted Hinckley aiming a small pistol. McCarthy, along with other agents and police officers, lunged through the crowd, landed on Hinckley, and pulled him to the ground.

Meanwhile, two other Secret Service agents grabbed President Reagan and shoved him to safety inside his armored limousine. The car sped away. Short of breath, the president began to cough up bright red blood. Jerry Parr, Secret Service special agent in charge (SAIC), realized the president had been shot. Parr gave orders to the driver of the car to go to George Washington University Hospital. Within three minutes, the president received life-saving medical care.

Three other people were hit by gunfire in the assassination attempt. All survived, thanks in no small part to the U.S. Secret Service. President Reagan also recovered from the attack. But without the quick and courageous response of agents Tim McCarthy, Dennis McCarthy, and Jerry Parr, the president's wounds would have been much more grave.

Such is the job of the U.S. Secret Service. As the law-enforcement agency that protects the president and other political notables, the Secret Service provides around-the-clock security for the nation's most important government officials.

The Secret Service was established on July 5, 1865, to combat counterfeiting, the act of making fake money. But the agency's responsibilities have expanded since then. Today, the Secret Service, which is part of the Treasury Department, employs 4,300 people in its continuing battle to safeguard the nation's money supply and protect the president and other important political figures from possible harm.

For example, Secret Service agents escort the president each time he leaves the White House. These brave men and women check rooftops for snipers. They inspect roads and airport runways for hidden bombs. Secret Service agents act as human shields—they walk next to the president while he is in public, and they jog alongside his limousine during parades and motorcades. Secret Service agents even accompany the president on vacation. If he skis, they patrol the slopes. If he scuba dives, they wear masks and oxygen tanks and swim underwater with him.

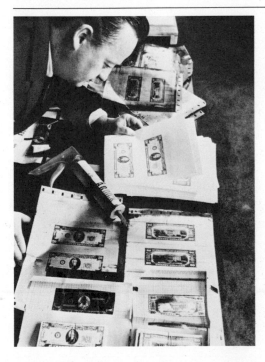

A Secret Service agent inspects a cache of counterfeit $20 bills, totaling $45,000, confiscated during a raid. The Secret Service was created in 1865 to investigate currency fraud.

But the president is not the only person the Secret Service must protect. By law and executive order, the Secret Service is responsible for the physical protection of the following persons: the president, vice-president, and their immediate families; the president-elect, vice-president-elect, and their immediate families; former presidents and their wives; the widow of a former president until her remarriage or death; minor children of a former president until they are 16 years old; major presidential and vice-presidential candidates; and visiting heads of a foreign state or a foreign government. At the direction of the president, other distinguished foreign visitors to the United States and official representatives of the United States performing special missions abroad are also safeguarded. Many hundreds, even thousands, of other people also benefit from the protection the Secret Service provides at such locations as the White House complex, the Treasury Department, buildings that house presidential-staff offices, various foreign diplomatic missions in the Washington, D.C., area, and other locations that the president may designate.

The second major responsibility of the Secret Service—the job for which it was created—is to protect the nation's currency. Originally this was primarily a matter of combating counterfeiting. Today, it is an immensely more complex task because money is no longer circulated simply in the form of paper bills and metal coins. Every day millions of dollars are exchanged among people and

An agent examines forged U.S. government checks. Each year check theft and forgery result in greater financial losses than counterfeiting because forgers do not need expensive equipment to practice their craft—only a stolen check and a pen. Unfortunately, many retailers cash government checks without carefully inspecting the identification of the endorser.

businesses by checks, credit cards, and similar methods. Billions more are transferred electronically, by computer links between banks, businesses, securities dealers, and financially active individuals. The Secret Service must be involved with many different aspects of monetary law enforcement.

Counterfeiting is by no means a thing of the past. Criminals throughout the world produce imitation U.S. currency to finance illegal activities. They use paper and ink similar to the kinds the government uses to make money. They mint coins and print bills that are nearly identical to the real thing. They also counterfeit credit cards, stocks, bonds, and other securities and checks, the use of which can undermine the value of our currency. To combat this problem, the Secret Service uses advanced chemical tests and other sophisticated analytical processes to determine whether money or other items are genuine or counterfeit. Such methods, along with intense field investigation and large-scale stakeouts, enable the service to catch counterfeiters.

As the nation's oldest general law-enforcement agency, the United States Secret Service is one of the best-trained security forces in the world. The agency's constant vigilance ensures that American leaders can do their jobs safely, with less fear of physical harm. The agency's watch over our money supply helps keep our economy strong and secure.

The front (obverse) and back (reverse) of colonial currency printed in 1776. At that time, the crime of counterfeiting was punishable by death.

TWO

The Birth of the Secret Service

Mention the Secret Service and most people think of the well-trained men and women who protect the president. But the agency was established in 1865 for a much different purpose: to protect the country's currency from counterfeiting.

To understand the threat counterfeiting poses, it is important to realize the significant role that hard currency plays in a nation's economy. Money represents the confidence shoppers and merchants hold in one another. If counterfeit currency becomes mixed with a country's genuine money, merchants stop conducting business for fear they may receive worthless paper or metal in exchange for valuable products.

Because of money's importance, only the United States government is permitted to mint coins and to print bills of any denomination in this country. But that was not always the case.

In the 1700s, before the revolutionary war, American colonists used English, Spanish, and French money. During the Revolution, the colonists issued their own paper money. Called Continental currency, the money took its design from a plate engraved by Paul Revere, the great patriot and silversmith.

Unfortunately, the British started counterfeiting the money in America and the currency soon became worthless, giving rise to the phrase, "not worth a Continental."

After the adoption of the U.S. Constitution in 1787, Congress authorized two U.S. federal banks to issue paper bills. By 1836, however, both banks had closed, and local banks operating under charters from individual states issued paper money in a variety of designs.

The lack of uniform currency became a serious problem during the Civil War, which lasted from 1861 to 1865. During these years, according to U.S. government estimates, there were about 1,600 state banks printing their own money, each with different designs. Complicating matters, the war drew attention away from civilian law enforcement. Many criminals began counterfeiting the various currencies to finance illegal activities. During the Civil War one out of every three bills in circulation was counterfeit.

To combat the problem, the government standardized its currency in 1863. The Treasury Department became the sole source of American currency and adopted a consistent shape, size, and color for paper money. Nevertheless, counterfeiting continued. After the Civil War ended in 1865, the national

A clerk accepts money from a customer in exchange for goods. Merchants should carefully inspect the currency they receive throughout a business day and cooperate with the Secret Service when counterfeiting is suspected.

A one-dollar bill, popularly called a greenback, issued by the U.S. Treasury in 1862. The Union intended to issue paper money during the Civil War only as a temporary measure to help solve its financial crisis.

currency was still being illegally copied with frightening regularity. Government officials, concerned that the practice would destroy the nation's economy, searched for ways to eliminate the problem.

In April 1865, President Abraham Lincoln listened as Treasury secretary Hugh McCulloch expressed the need for a federal agency to combat counterfeiting. McCulloch told Lincoln that the U.S. government had tried everything in its power to control the problem without much success. The only solution, McCulloch said, was "a continuous organized effort . . . undertaken by a permanent force managed by a directing head."

Lincoln agreed, and McCulloch set about establishing the Secret Service. It is ironic that Lincoln approved the plan on April 14, 1865; on the evening of that same day, the president was fatally shot by John Wilkes Booth. But the wheels were already set in motion that would establish an agency to protect presidents in the future.

Lincoln's death disrupted the government for many months. But once things returned to normal, the Secret Service was established as a small division within the Treasury Department. On July 5, 1865, William P. Wood, a former soldier and government official, became the first chief of the Secret Service.

At the modest ceremony, Edward P. Jordan, solicitor of the Treasury, swore Wood in and then remarked, "The main objective is to restore public confidence in the money of this country."

Wood recruited 10 "operatives," as early Secret Service agents were called. Many were former private detectives or soldiers who had served in the Union

23

Hugh McCulloch, appointed secretary of the Treasury by President Abraham Lincoln in 1865, persuaded Lincoln to establish the Secret Service to fight counterfeiting.

army during the Civil War. The agents fanned out across the country into 11 districts, setting up field offices in large cities, small towns, and anywhere else counterfeiters were suspected of operating.

From the beginning, the Secret Service won a name for discipline and dedication. Chief Wood issued a set of six General Orders that spelled out each agent's allegiance to the service and his legal and moral obligations. These first orders read

1. Each man must recognize that his service belongs to the government 24 hours of every day.

2. All must agree to assignment to the locations chosen by the Chief and respond to whatever mobility of movement the work might require.

3. All must exercise such careful saving of money spent for travel, subsistence, and payments for information as can be self-evidently justified.

4. Continuing employment in the Service will depend upon demonstrated fitness, ability as investigators, and honesty and fidelity in all transactions.

5. The title of regular employees will be Operative, Secret Service. Temporary employees will be Assistant Operatives or Informants.

6. All employment will be at a daily pay rate; accounts submitted monthly.

Each operative will be expected to keep on hand enough personal reserve funds to carry on Service business between pay days.

The emphasis in these orders on fidelity to the service and on scrupulous financial honesty were very important matters to Wood. In the mid-1860s, when the Secret Service was formed, law enforcement in general did not have a good reputation. This was due in part to the disruptions caused by the Civil War, but primarily it was because organized law enforcement was still in its infancy. The first metropolitan police department in the country had been established only in 1844, in New York City. Other cities followed suit, but most departments were essentially private organizations drawing money from the public treasury with little accountability. Some were little more than uniformed gangs whose officers were cronies of political party bosses or city officials who were often corrupt. Private investigators seem to have been even worse in many cases. There were virtually no laws to establish their qualifications, licensing, or authority or to regulate their conduct. Many investigators were interested only in gaining information that they could turn to personal profit and would not hesitate to blackmail a client or betray him to his opponents.

William Wood was determined to establish an agency that would be above reproach and never be touched by even the slightest hint of scandal. The general orders to Secret Service agents have been modified and expanded as the organization has grown more complex and has been given ever-increasing areas of responsibility. But the principles embodied in that first set of orders are valid today and all agents adhere to them faithfully.

To perform their jobs, agents in the early days distributed circulars explaining their duties to law-enforcement officers throughout the country. They received many tips regarding counterfeiting and set up stakeouts to catch the criminals. In its first year of operation, the Secret Service apprehended 200 of the United States's most notorious counterfeiters and confiscated hundreds of thousands of dollars in counterfeit currency.

But for all its early effectiveness, the Secret Service failed initially to capture William E. Brockway, known at the time as the "King of the Counterfeiters." Brockway was personally responsible for producing hundreds of thousands of counterfeit dollars. He also forged U.S. government bonds. (The U.S. Department of the Treasury sells different types of bonds to the public as investment certificates. Bonds help finance the government's expenses; some bonds pay interest to the buyer while others increase in value over time.)

Brockway learned to counterfeit in the late 1830s while an apprentice to a printer in New Haven, Connecticut. At the time, banks still printed their own currency. The print shop in which Brockway worked printed money for the New Haven City Bank. The bank's owner always supervised the printing process to make sure nothing was done improperly.

But Brockway spotted a criminal opportunity, and he enlisted the help of the print shop owner, Ezra Becker. While Brockway was printing the bank's money, Becker distracted the bank owner long enough for Brockway to copy the bank's printing plates. Brockway used a thick sheet of lead to form an illegal impression of the plate's engravings. From the impressions, Brockway and Becker made duplicate plates and printed $100,000 worth of counterfeit $5 bills. Brockway forged the bank owner's signature on every bill.

A bank teller soon noticed the irregular signature and a police investigation ensued. Brockway fled Connecticut, was later arrested in New York, and was convicted, but spent less than a year in jail.

Upon his release, he and his wife moved to Philadelphia, where they bought a large home. They assumed the names "Colonel and Mrs. William E. Spencer." The neighbors considered Spencer/Brockway a respectable businessman. In reality, however, he and a partner, James B. Doyle, had established an elaborate counterfeiting ring that employed highly skilled engravers.

By 1865, the ring concentrated on forging U.S. bonds issued to finance Reconstruction after the Civil War. So precise were the counterfeit bonds that the Department of Treasury actually redeemed some of the bonds, believing them to be authentic. The counterfeits were discovered when a Treasury Department employee noticed two bonds with the same serial number (no two genuine bonds are ever issued with the same serial number). But the bonds looked so authentic that many Treasury Department employees thought the U.S. Government Printing Office must have made a mistake.

Treasury secretary McCulloch soon heard about the discrepancy and called Secret Service chief Wood into his office. Two bonds lay on McCulloch's desk. Wood picked up the notes, inspected them with a magnifying glass, and pronounced the forged one counterfeit.

McCulloch called for immediate action. He offered a $20,000 reward to anyone, including Secret Service agents, who uncovered the counterfeit printing plates.

Wood heeded the call. He knew about Brockway's criminal career and believed the counterfeiter produced excellent quality work. After two weeks of investigation, Wood determined that Brockway was living in Philadelphia as Colonel Spencer. He interviewed neighbors and discovered that Brockway was by then in New York City preparing for a European vacation.

A U.S. attorney inspects a counterfeiting plant seized by the Secret Service in Pennsylvania during the mid-1940s.

Wood traveled to New York and confronted Brockway and his wife at their hotel. Brockway insisted his name was Spencer, and that he was not involved in counterfeiting. Wood knew better. He moved the couple to a New Jersey hotel and questioned them for five straight days.

"I kept him on tenterhooks day and night," Wood later said. "Our interviews were continuous and spicy—and by the evidence I put before him he finally admitted that he was Brockway, the former New Haven counterfeiter."

Brockway later surrendered the counterfeit plates and provided testimony that allowed the Secret Service to gain the convictions of others involved with the ring. He received a suspended sentence and continued his life of crime. The Secret Service again apprehended Brockway, at age 74, for counterfeiting government bonds. This time, he received a 10-year sentence.

Wood retired as chief of the Secret Service in 1869 to investigate other cases related to Brockway's counterfeit bond scheme. The efficiency Wood displayed in apprehending Brockway provided an early model for Secret Service agents to follow.

A late 19th-century illustration of Abraham Lincoln's tomb in Springfield, Illinois. The Secret Service thwarted a plot to kidnap the former president's body and hold it for ransom.

THREE

Growth and Development

During the late 1800s, the U.S. government frequently called upon the Secret Service to help investigate other crimes besides counterfeiting.

Perhaps the most bizarre investigation occurred in 1887 when the Secret Service learned about a plot to rob Abraham Lincoln's tomb while they were investigating a counterfeiting ring in the Chicago area. Ben Boyd, an expert counterfeiter, had been arrested and sentenced to 10 years in an Indiana prison. However, counterfeit bills with Boyd's tell-tale signs of mastery continued to appear in the Chicago area. The Secret Service believed that two of Boyd's friends, Terence Mullen and Jack Hughes, were passing fake money that Boyd had printed before going to prison.

To aid in the investigation of the counterfeiters, the Secret Service enlisted the help of an informant named Lou Swigles. Swigles, upon the urging of the Secret Service, won the friendship of Mullen and Hughes, who told Swigles that they indeed continued to pass Boyd's counterfeit bills. But their supply was dwindling, and they needed to get Boyd out of prison to print more. They then described how they planned to accomplish this goal.

Mullen and Hughes would travel to Springfield, Illinois, where former president Lincoln's body was entombed. They planned to break into the tomb at night, remove the body, and transport it by horse-drawn carriage to Indiana. There, they would re-bury Lincoln and then demand Boyd's release as ransom for return of the body. Mullen and Hughes wanted Swigles to take part in the conspiracy.

Instead, Swigles quickly reported the scheme to Patrick D. Tyrrell, Special Agent in Charge (SAIC) of the Secret Service's Chicago field office. At first, Tyrrell refused to believe the bizarre story. But Swigles provided so many details that the agency was convinced that it should act.

The Secret Service did not have jurisdiction or legal authority to investigate a grave robbery. So Tyrrell contacted his supervisors in Washington, D.C., for instructions. They suggested he tell the story to Robert Lincoln, the former president's only surviving son, who lived in Chicago.

Tyrrell explained the details of the plot to Lincoln who, outraged, requested the Secret Service's assistance in stopping the crime. This request provided some legal basis for the service to take action. Tyrrell devised a plan to catch the grave robbers. He told Swigles to play along with Mullen and Hughes and travel to Springfield, Illinois, as if nothing had happened.

Tyrrell faced another problem. Because the Secret Service was severely short of manpower, he was the only agent available to go to Springfield, but one man would not be enough. At the urging of Robert Lincoln, Tyrrell contacted Allan Pinkerton, a well-known private detective who had been a personal friend of Abraham Lincoln's. Pinkerton chose two of his best private detectives to help Tyrrell. Tyrrell was also able to enlist the aid of a retired Secret Service agent and two Chicago detectives.

The six men trailed Mullen, Hughes, and Swigles to Springfield. The conspirators cased the cemetery where Lincoln's body rested and asked the gravekeeper many questions. They wanted to know the weight of the casket and how the tomb was protected. Swigles secretly contacted SAIC Tyrrell and told him when Mullen and Hughes planned to commit the crime.

On the night of the robbery, the investigators arrived at the cemetery just before 7 o'clock and hid about 200 feet from Lincoln's tomb. Ninety minutes later, the conspirators showed up and began sawing through the tomb's padlock.

After 30 minutes, Swigles left Mullen and Hughes on the pretext of checking out the horse-drawn carriage and driver. But there was no carriage. In reality, Swigles reported to Tyrrell and told him the thieves were almost through the padlock.

President William McKinley was fatally shot by anarchist Leon Czolgosz on September 6, 1901, while touring the Pan-American Exposition in Buffalo, New York. Secret Service agents caught Czolgosz before he could escape.

Tyrrell ordered his men to advance toward the tomb. But as they approached it, one of the detectives' guns accidentally discharged, warning Mullen and Hughes of someone's presence.

By the time the investigators reached the tomb, the two thieves had fled. Tyrrell and his men searched the cemetery without success. The next day, they patrolled the train station but again came up empty-handed.

Disappointed but not discouraged, Tyrrell returned to Chicago and discovered that Hughes was also back in town. The Secret Service staked out his apartment. When Hughes returned they did not arrest him, but waited in hiding. As they hoped, the unsuspecting Hughes soon led the investigators to Mullen and both men were arrested. The next day the two thieves were returned to Springfield to be charged with their attempted crime. After a two-day trial, the court found the pair guilty and sentenced them both to a year in prison.

The Lincoln tomb plot was the first time the Secret Service had been involved in matters concerning a president. Fourteen years later a more tragic

Snapshots of Leon Czolgosz taken shortly after his arrest.

crime served to shape the duties of the service for many years to come.

On September 6, 1901, President William McKinley was shot and killed by Leon F. Czolgosz (pronounced *chol-gosh*). Czolgosz was an intelligent man who grew up in Michigan and worked in a wire factory near Cleveland, Ohio. At the time, America was in the middle of the Industrial Revolution, which saw the development of the factory system of production. Many factory laborers worked long hours for little pay. To combat unfair working conditions, some workers banded together to form unions, which presented their grievances to factory owners. Other workers, however, explored more radical alternatives, including anarchism, a political philosophy that supports the elimination of all governmental control over individuals.

In 1893, the Cleveland wire factory workers went on strike for higher wages. Czolgosz, whose family was religious, prayed that the strike would be settled in favor of the workers. His prayers went unanswered, and Czolgosz renounced his religion and began reading about radical political philosophies. After suffering a mental and physical breakdown, Czolgosz became attracted to the philosophy of anarchism in 1900 when an anarchist, Gaetano Bresci, assassinated Italian King Humbert I.

Czolgosz studied newspaper accounts of the murder with great interest. Soon he began plotting a similar murder of President William McKinley. He even contacted a leader of an American anarchist organization in 1901 to inquire whether its members planned to assassinate McKinley.

Alarmed by the question, the anarchist club ran an announcement in its newspaper warning members to stay clear of Czolgosz. But no one reported his activities to the police. Even if the police had been alerted, there was no federal agency to investigate individuals who posed a threat to the president of the United States.

Complicating matters, Czolgosz soon disappeared from Cleveland and resurfaced in Buffalo, New York. That summer, the city was host to the Pan-American Exposition, an international fair. Coincidentally, President McKinley announced that he would visit the exposition the first week in September.

Czolgosz saw the opportunity to kill the president. He bought a .38-caliber pistol in late August and followed McKinley during his visit to the exposition. Czolgosz was particularly angered by the respect shown the president. "I thought it wasn't right for one man to get so much ceremony," Czolgosz later said. "I saw a great many people there saluting him, bowing to him, paying homage to him and honoring the president."

At the time, the Secret Service was not officially in charge of protecting the president. However, three Secret Service agents went along on the trip. Agents often traveled with McKinley on special assignment, helping to arrange his personal appearances.

Security was lax on the day of the shooting even though many of the president's advisers were concerned for his safety during public appearances. They asked McKinley to cancel a public reception scheduled for the exposition's main pavilion, but he replied, "Why should I? No one would wish to hurt me."

At the reception Czolgosz was one of the hundreds who waited in line to meet the president. Around his hand he had wrapped a white handkerchief to conceal the pistol he had bought only days before.

The line moved slowly, and Czolgosz inched steadily toward the president. When the two men finally met face to face, Czolgosz slapped aside McKinley's outstretched hand and fired two shots through the handkerchief. The first bullet hit the president in his chest. The second ripped through his stomach.

Secret Service agents hit Czolgosz and knocked him to the floor. Confusion reigned for a moment as others struck Czolgosz.

McKinley was rushed to a nearby hospital and underwent immediate surgery. During the next few days, his condition appeared to improve. But eight days after the shooting, the president's health took a dramatic turn for the worse, and he died.

Czolgosz was tried and found guilty of first-degree murder. On October 29, 1901, he was strapped in the electric chair and executed. "I am not sorry for my crimes," were his last words.

The assassination marked the third time an American president had been killed in 36 years. (Lincoln was murdered in 1865 and James Garfield was shot and killed by a disappointed office-seeker in 1881.) The presidency had become a dangerous job.

McKinley's death was made more tragic by the fact that it could have been prevented. Many people had heard Czolgosz threaten the life of the president, but nothing was done. Moreover, tighter security at the Pan-American Exposition might have discovered Czolgosz's concealed gun and prevented the assassination.

The public cried out for an effective means of protecting the president. In response, Theodore Roosevelt, shortly after succeeding McKinley as president, assigned the Secret Service to provide around-the-clock protection for the president. In 1906, Congress formalized the responsibility by providing funds specifically for this purpose under the Sundry Civil Expenses Act. Protection of the highest office in the land was now the priority for the men and women of the Secret Service.

Since 1906, the agency's protective responsibilities have increased steadily. In 1913, Secret Service protection was extended to the president-elect. In 1917, the president's immediate family gained Secret Service protection. In 1951, Secret Service protection was afforded to the vice-president and his family upon request.

In 1962, Congress further broadened the Secret Service's duties by providing protection to the vice-president and his family (without special request) or other officeholder in the immediate line of succession to the presidency. Congress also passed legislation to provide protection for the vice-president-elect, as well as for former presidents upon their request for a reasonable period after leaving office.

After the assassination of President Kennedy in 1963, the law was again changed to extend Secret Service protection (without request) to former presidents, their spouses, widows, and children until age 16. After Senator

Robert Kennedy was assassinated while campaigning for his party's nomination to the presidency in 1968, Congress extended the Secret Service's duties to protecting candidates for the offices of president and vice-president, and within 120 days of the presidential election, their spouses. Today, the Secret Service also guards visiting heads of foreign states and other individuals upon the president's request.

Although much attention is paid to the Secret Service's responsibilities to the president, the agency is greatly concerned with the protection of the president's immediate family—generally referred to as the first family.

In this capacity, Secret Service agents accompany family members everywhere they go. Agents stay near them while shopping or attending school. They accompany family members on vacations and even honeymoons, guarding against possible kidnapping or attempted assassination.

One of the most dangerous incidents agents encountered occurred in 1958 when Vice-president Richard M. Nixon and his wife toured South America. It was a turbulent time in the region and anti-American sentiment ran high. In

Agents surround Theodore Roosevelt (seated in carriage) on the way to his inauguration as president in 1901. Congress responded to the public outcry for increased protection of the president after McKinley's assassination by allotting funds to the Secret Service so that it could provide around-the-clock protection.

Peru, 2,000 students turned out to shout "Muera Nixon," Spanish for "Death to Nixon." During the demonstration, Nixon was hit on the arm with a rock. Another stone struck Secret Service agent John Sherwood in the mouth and dislodged a front tooth.

In addition to Sherwood, 13 other Secret Service agents were with Nixon. None realized the danger they would soon face in Venezuela. Five months before Nixon's visit to that country a political coup had sent Marcos Pérez Jiménez, Venezuela's hated dictator, fleeing to the United States. The United States granted Jiménez political asylum, allowing him to live safely in this country.

The Venezuelan people were outraged by the U.S. action and intended to vent their anger on Vice-president Nixon and his wife. When Nixon's airplane landed in Caracas, Venezuela's capital city, hundreds of protesters showed up to shout anti-American slogans. As the vice-president and his wife stood beneath the airport's observation deck, the crowd spat on them and screamed "Go, go, go!"

A violent mob engulfs Vice-president Richard M. Nixon's limousine during his visit to Caracas, Venezuela, in 1958. After the incident, Secret Service protection of vice-presidents was tightened.

When Nixon tried to enter a limousine, the crowd surged forward to stop him. Secret Service agents formed a circle around him and his wife and nudged their way through the mob.

Once in the car, the vice-president planned to become part of a motorcade that would visit the grave of Simón Bolívar, the great Latin American soldier and statesman who helped six nations win freedom from Spanish rule. But as the cars passed through the streets of Caracas, they were greeted by rock-throwing demonstrators. Four blocks from Bolívar's grave, protesters pulled a dump truck in front of the motorcade to block the roadway. The limousines stopped, and an angry mob, wielding lead pipes and stones, charged toward them.

The mob beat on the car's shatterproof windows, sending tiny slivers of glass through the interior of the cars.

The limousines were lined up bumper-to-bumper in an attempt to discourage protesters from climbing on top of the cars. But demonstrators kept attacking from the sides. One protester beat on Nixon's window until the glass broke, showering the vice-president with glass.

The angry crowd began to rock the cars up and down in an attempt to overturn them. Such mobs had been known to flip automobiles and then set them on fire with the occupants still inside.

The scene continued for several minutes. The Secret Service agents fingered their automatic weapons, considering whether to open fire. Just before violence erupted, however, the Venezuelan army appeared. They opened a path through the rioters and the motorcade sped to safety down Caracas's back streets.

Nixon, his wife, their advisers, and Secret Service agents were later moved safely out of the country. But the incident exposed many problems in Secret Service planning and preparations that were corrected in the future: The number of agents assigned to protect the vice-president was significantly increased, and the Secret Service began to work more closely with other agencies gathering information regarding foreign governments.

But the changes did little to prevent one of the greatest tragedies in American history—the assassination of President John F. Kennedy in 1963. Elected president in 1960, for many people Kennedy represented a new beginning in America. Young and vibrant, he came to symbolize the potential that the United States possessed. That made his death all the more traumatic to the American people.

In an effort to understand the tragedy, the nation underwent a period of self-evaluation. People questioned the events leading up to the assassination.

Secret Service agent Clinton J. Hill pushes First Lady Jacqueline Kennedy back into the limousine moments after President John F. Kennedy was shot in Dallas, Texas, on November 22, 1963.

Was the killing part of a larger, international conspiracy? Who was to blame?

Of course, the Secret Service fell under heavy criticism because it was the agency's responsibility to protect the life of the president. Many Americans assumed that the Secret Service must have been derelict in its duty.

But in the investigation following the assassination, recorded in the Warren Commission Report, the Secret Service was absolved of much blame. (The Warren Commission was created by President Lyndon B. Johnson to investigate Kennedy's death and the subsequent murder of alleged assassin Lee Harvey Oswald. The chairman of the commission was Earl Warren, chief justice of the Supreme Court.) Although the Commission identified specific areas where the Secret Service needed to improve, it also concluded that the service had adequately performed many of its responsibilities.

The Warren Commission Report stated: "This commission can recommend no procedures for the future protection of our President which will guarantee security. The demands on the President in the execution of his responsibilities in today's world are so varied and complex and the traditions of the office in a

38

democracy such as ours are so deep-seated as to preclude absolute security."

The Warren Commission also uncovered no evidence of a larger conspiracy in the assassination of Kennedy. Instead, the investigators placed the sole blame on Lee Harvey Oswald, a mysterious man who had a record of mental instability. In 1956, Oswald had joined the U.S. Marines, becoming an expert marksman. He often angered other marines by reciting communist philosophies. After his discharge, Oswald moved briefly to the Soviet Union and met and married a Soviet citizen, Marina Nikolaevna.

But Oswald soon became disillusioned with Soviet life and returned to the United States with his new bride and infant daughter in 1962. The family lived in New Orleans, Louisiana, until domestic problems caused Marina to move to Dallas, Texas. Oswald soon followed her and found a job as a clerk at the Texas School Book Depository in downtown Dallas.

In the interim, Oswald also purchased an Italian-made rifle from a mail-order sporting goods firm.

Although the Federal Bureau of Investigation (FBI) was well aware of Lee Harvey Oswald's peculiar background, the Secret Service was not. When the service was notified that President Kennedy would visit Dallas on November 22, 1963, it concentrated on securing a building for the testimonial luncheon

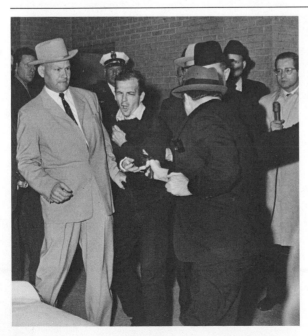

Dallas nightclub owner Jack Ruby fatally shoots accused assassin Lee Harvey Oswald two days after President Kennedy's assassination.

Agents Clinton J. Hill, Roy Kellerman, and William Greer after testifying before the Warren Commission, which investigated President Kennedy's assassination.

and mapping a safe route for the presidential motorcade. Not knowing about Oswald's history, the agency did not place him under surveillance.

Once the site for the luncheon was selected by the president's staff, the motorcade route was chosen. It wound around downtown Dallas and passed close to the Texas School Book Depository building.

The week before Kennedy arrived, tensions were high in the city. Although Kennedy's vice-president, Lyndon Johnson, was from Texas, the president, a liberal, faced fierce political opposition in Dallas, a conservative stronghold. In fact, the day before Kennedy's visit, handbills were distributed throughout the city accusing the president of treason. Dallas newspapers also ran harsh criticisms of the president.

Kennedy was undeterred by the hostility. On the morning of November 22, the president spoke with reporters about Texas's role in national defense. "This is a very dangerous and uncertain world," he said.

At about the same time, Oswald was accepting a ride to work from a friend. In his arms, he carried a large bundle wrapped in brown paper; he told his friend it contained curtain rods. Investigators later established that Oswald was carrying the mail-order rifle that morning.

A motorcade met Kennedy at Carswell Air Force Base at about noon. Kennedy and his wife Jacqueline sat in the backseat. Also in the car were Texas governor John Connally, his wife, and Secret Service agents Roy H. Kellerman and William R. Greer. Greer was driving.

Two details of motorcycle police led the procession. Behind Kennedy's limousine, four Secret Service agents followed in a specially designed Cadillac convertible. Four other agents rode on the car's running boards. The agents carried many weapons.

But for all the firepower, there was little the Secret Service could do as the motorcade passed the Texas School Book Depository and shots rang out.

After hearing the first blast, Agent Kellerman turned and saw the president clutching his throat. At the same moment Agent Clinton J. Hill jumped from the running board of the convertible, ran to the rear of the president's limousine, and climbed on top of the trunk. Two more shots rang out. "Let's get out of here; we are hit," Agent Kellerman shouted to the president's driver. Hill managed to keep the first lady from falling out of the car as it leapt forward. Without Hill's quick action, Jacqueline Kennedy might have been shot or seriously injured.

The motorcade raced to Parkland Hospital, where a team of physicians had already been notified by radio of the president's injuries. Unfortunately, there was nothing they could do. Kennedy had suffered massive head injuries and was soon pronounced dead.

Governor Connally was also hit by gunfire. After a series of operations, he recovered.

Lee Harvey Oswald was apprehended shortly after the shooting in the back row of a Dallas movie theater. In his haste to escape, Oswald had also killed a police officer. Two days later, Oswald's life met a violent end when Jack Ruby, a Dallas nightclub owner, burst from a crowd of reporters and shot and killed Oswald in front of television cameras. Ruby claimed to have murdered Oswald to protect Jacqueline Kennedy. He believed that with Oswald dead, the first lady would not have to relive the events of November 22, 1963, as a witness at Oswald's murder trial.

In the aftermath of Kennedy's death, the Secret Service increased its manpower significantly, as recommended by the Warren Commission. The agency also drastically revamped the criteria it employed to identify persons who posed threats to the president.

The Warren Report also forced the Secret Service to improve the strategies it used to protect political figures in motorcades. In cities across the country, the agency identified buildings that could house snipers. These buildings are now carefully inspected and guarded during a politician's visit to the area.

As a result, in part, of these more stringent methods, no government official under Secret Service protection has been assassinated since 1963.

A Secret Service agent holds on to President Nixon as he leans over to shake hands with tourists visiting the White House.

FOUR

Inside the Organization

Today, the U.S. Secret Service is one of the most sophisticated law-enforcement agencies in the world. Over the last century and a quarter it has refined its duties to needle sharpness. The Secret Service is responsible for investigating the counterfeiting of U.S. currency and other financial obligations and securities of the United States. It is also responsible for investigating the theft, trafficking, and forgery of U.S. checks, bonds, and other financial certificates issued by the government. In 1984, Congress passed legislation that expanded the agency's duties to include investigating credit card and computer fraud. At the direction of the secretary of the Treasury, the Secret Service is also authorized to investigate fraud related to the electronic funds transfer system (EFTS) of the Department of the Treasury. In this system, money is transmitted electronically from one account to another by using computers.

More and more, electronic funds are replacing paper money in the U.S. economy. Consumer goods paid for with credit cards and borrowing credit extended by banks are two examples of funds transfers that do *not* involve paper money. Instead, advanced computers keep track of bits of information that represent money. Many of the computer systems also manage large funds transfers made by the Treasury Department to regional banks and other major financial institutions. To protect these systems against possible illegal practices, Secret Service employees work with other computer and financial experts to closely monitor the computers, review printouts, and search for irregularities. If something appears improper, they launch an investigation, which could include questioning the people involved, extending surveillance over certain individuals, or even placing undercover agents within a suspected organization. Much of what the Secret Service does with regard to currency matters requires the cooperation of other Treasury Department divisions such as the Bureau of Engraving and Printing, U.S. Mint, U.S. Customs Service, Internal Revenue Service, and the U.S. Savings Bond Division.

To accomplish its dual investigative and protective roles—guarding the nation's money supply and its key officials—the Secret Service headquarters staff is divided into nine separate offices.

The Office of Protective Research

The Office of Protective Research is composed of a number of smaller divisions that search for innovative methods of protecting important government officials. The office's Technical Security Division develops sophisticated alarm systems and evaluates innovative pass systems that are used to identify government employees.

The Office of Protective Research is also responsible for collecting, processing, and evaluating information about individuals who may pose a threat to the president. Every year the Secret Service receives a large number of threats against the president. Many are made by apparent cranks but are still given careful evaluation. Others are taken even more seriously. For example, if the threat is typewritten, investigators in the Office of Protective Research examine the print under microscopes. From the printed impression, they often determine the make and year of the typewriter used. The investigators then check their records for similar threats made on similar machines. In some instances, their careful scrutiny can identify the culprit.

During the administration of Dwight D. Eisenhower, a note was received at the White House threatening the life of the president. The letter was mailed from a small town in Arkansas. Careful inspection showed that the typewriter's letter *o* had a slight crack in it. The information was passed on to postal employees in the town. Six months later, the postmaster noticed an envelope with a similar cracked letter *o*. He contacted the Secret Service, and agents discovered the letter writer—a severely disturbed woman. After proper legal proceedings she was committed to a mental institution.

Today, the Office of Protective Research is composed of professionals from many walks of life, including computer experts, electronics engineers, communications technicians, research psychologists, intelligence analysts, lie-detector operators, and agents trained in more general investigative practices.

The Offices of Protective Operations and Investigation

Just as important as the Office of Protective Research are the Office of Protective Operations and the Office of Investigation. Together, these two branches of the Secret Service perform the primary duties of the agency: The Office of Protective Operations deals mainly with safeguarding the president and other government officials and dignitaries; the Office of Investigation employs its resources to combat counterfeiting including currency, government checks and bonds, and commercial credit cards. The Office of Investigation also

A restaurant owner in Traverse City, Michigan, shows the counterfeit $20 bill he received from a customer. Altering currency to increase its value is punishable by a fine of up to $5,000, 15 years' imprisonment, or both.

Golda Meir (left), prime minister of Israel, walks with President Nixon (right) during a visit to the White House. A Secret Service agent follows close behind, scanning the crowd to assure the officials' safety.

supervises the operations of the service's field offices, such as their criminal investigations and the gathering of protective intelligence.

The jobs of both offices are performed by employees called special agents, who provide a wide variety of services from 110 different locations throughout the United States. For example, some special agents provide temporary security for visiting officials from foreign countries. Special agents have protected the queen of England, the pope, and other dignitaries. Other special agents hold permanent assignments. These agents protect the president and vice-president and their families, sometimes staying with them for several years.

The most prestigious position for a special agent is in the Presidential Protective Division. Agents in this division travel throughout the world, making sure that the nation's top official is safe. And when the president is at home in Washington, D.C., they stand constant watch to ensure that the president and his family are secure.

Special agents of the Presidential Protective Division, surprisingly, do not answer to the president. They work for the Secret Service, which in turn answers to the secretary of the Treasury.

Special agents outside Washington are assigned to Secret Service field offices. The field offices serve as the Secret Service operational centers, each for a specific geographical area. There are 63 field offices throughout the United States. In addition, the Secret Service maintains approximately 49 resident agent offices that provide the same services as field offices but for smaller geographic areas.

Special agents stationed at field offices and resident agent offices perform both protective and investigative assignments. For instance, if the president should visit the area, special agents of the particular field office supplement the Presidential Protective Division's efforts in protecting the president. The same situation holds true for other officials who receive Secret Service protection.

To investigate fraud and counterfeiting, field office special agents work closely with local police departments and citizens to initiate investigations. The agents employ a wide range of tactics to apprehend criminals. For example, they may assume undercover roles, befriending suspected criminals and gaining information regarding these persons' illegal activities. The Secret Service may also use hidden cameras or microphones to record the activities of counterfeiters. Agents will spend days, weeks, and months tracking the trail of a criminal. They meet with merchants who have innocently accepted counterfeit bills and ask for descriptions of the person who passed the bad money. Agents will then share this information with local law-enforcement officials as well as with other government agencies. The Secret Service stays on the case until it is solved. Of the 9,738 people arrested by the Secret Service in 1986, 95.6 percent, or 9,318, were convicted.

Another branch of the Secret Service's Office of Protective Operations is the Uniformed Division, which is responsible primarily for protecting the White House and other buildings that contain offices of the president and vice-president.

As their department's name suggests, the officers of the Uniformed Division wear full uniforms and openly display their weapons. This helps distinguish them from special agents, who wear street clothes and conceal their weapons beneath suit jackets or other clothing.

Stationed in Washington, D.C., the Uniformed Division traces its history to 1922, when it was established by President Warren G. Harding as an independent law-enforcement agency called the White House Police Force. In 1930, it became part of the Secret Service by order of President Herbert

Boats filled with Secret Service agents maneuver around President Reagan's boat (center) as he travels to a meeting during an economic summit conference in Venice, Italy. Agents safeguard the president in his travels throughout the world.

Secret Service agents use binoculars to continually check around a house where President Ford is visiting. Agents plan tight security measures with local officials before arriving at their destination.

Hoover, and in 1977 its name became the Uniformed Division. The Uniformed Division has served as the first line of defense against intruders into the White House for many years. Today, its presence is still strongly evident in and around the president's home. Officers of the division are always stationed at the gates of the White House, at strategic positions on the grounds, and inside the building.

As criminal methods become more sophisticated, so also do the procedures used to apprehend the perpetrators. At the White House entrances, officers of

49

Presidential candidate Jimmy Carter and Secret Service agents are followed by newsmen upon Carter's arrival in Los Angeles for a campaign visit. Since the death of Senator Robert F. Kennedy in 1968, all presidential and vice-presidential candidates have been protected by the agency.

the Uniformed Division operate machines to detect concealed weapons. They also use canine teams to respond to bomb threats, delivery of suspicious packages, and other situations where dogs can sniff out explosives.

Uniformed Division officers also conduct tours of the White House and give lectures about the building's history and furnishings.

In 1970, Congress increased the Uniformed Division's protective responsibilities to include security for foreign diplomatic missions in the Washington, D.C., area after the community requested protection against rising criminal assaults and other violence.

Today, the Uniformed Division provides security for the president and vice-president and their immediate families; the White House and grounds; the official residence of the vice-president; buildings in which presidential offices are located; and foreign diplomatic missions in the Washington, D.C., area and in other areas at the president's request.

The Office of Training

The Office of Training is responsible for teaching special agents and Uniformed Division officers the special skills they will need throughout their careers. Each new Secret Service recruit undergoes about two months of extensive training at the Federal Law Enforcement Training Center in Glynco, Georgia, and another two months at the Secret Service's own training facilities in the Washington, D.C., area. There, agents receive expert instruction in methods of detecting counterfeit money.

Agents also learn strategies for protecting the president and other dignitaries. They are taught crowd control, weapons handling, and communication technologies, as well as how to recognize people who pose potential threats to the people they protect.

During training, agents spend their time learning specialized skills needed in criminal investigation and developing their physical fitness. Because the job of a Secret Service agent is physically demanding, agents are expected to maintain their strength and stamina throughout their careers. In fact, agents are tested once every three months to assure physical fitness. The Office of Training requires that agents engage in frequent and regular exercise, such as running, calisthenics, weight lifting, and karate.

The Office of Administration

Like any large organization, the Secret Service needs people to make policy and rules, deal with administrative problems, pay the bills, and manage the staff. Located at the Secret Service headquarters in Washington, D.C., the Office of Administration oversees personnel, wage, and supply functions, enabling Secret Service employees to perform their jobs more efficiently.

The Office of Chief Counsel

The Office of Chief Counsel provides legal advice for the Secret Service. Every day, the Secret Service deals with a wide variety of people, from the general public to government officials and notorious criminals. Organizations that have this range of exposure are often called upon to legally account for their actions. The Office of Chief Counsel gives agents advice about criminal law during investigations and clarifies procedures involving administrative matters. When the Secret Service began its polygraph program (giving lie detector tests to job applicants) the program was carefully reviewed first by the Office of Chief Counsel to establish whether the rights of the individual were being infringed upon or not. The Office of Chief Counsel does not represent the Secret Service in legal proceedings—the attorney general's office in the Justice Department does—but the Office of Chief Counsel is responsible for supplying the supporting documents needed by the attorney general's office while defending the Secret Service in court. For instance, if an agent were involved in an automobile accident, the Office of Chief Counsel would complete all the paperwork required by the Justice Department.

The Office of Public Affairs

The Office of Public Affairs answers inquiries and issues written statements regarding the day-to-day operation of the agency. The agents assigned to Public Affairs are responsible for keeping the news media up-to-date on Secret Service activities. The Office of Public Affairs also develops brochures about employment opportunities and general information for distribution to the public.

The Office of Inspection

The Office of Inspection is an internal tracking team that polices Secret Service activities. The office routinely audits or inspects the financial records of field offices to monitor the use of government money allotted by Congress. Officials of the Office of Inspection also investigate other agencies in the Treasury Department upon the request of appropriate government officials.

The Liaison Office

Because of the Secret Service's many responsibilities, the agency must often work in cooperation with other government agencies. The Liaison Office aids in this process. For example, when the Secret Service identifies a suspected counterfeiter, the agency often contacts the Internal Revenue Service (IRS), which tracks an individual's income for tax purposes. The IRS tells the Secret Service how much earned income the suspect reported on recent tax returns. If this amount is insufficient to support the suspect's life-style, the Secret Service may assume that the suspect is supplementing his income through illegal activity—possibly counterfeiting.

Increasingly since World War II, crime in the United States has had international connections. This is true of monetary crime and of terrorist plots that may be aimed at U.S. government officials, especially the president. To deal with this aspect of criminal investigation, the Secret Service communicates with the International Criminal Police Organization, known as Interpol.

The headquarters of Interpol is in St. Cloud, France, a suburb of Paris. The organization's principal purpose is to provide information on the whereabouts of

The badge of the Uniformed Division of the Secret Service, as it appears on one of the division's cars.

criminals who have crossed national borders and to promote scientific crime-detection and investigation.

Each member country designates an agency or governmental body to be its link with Interpol and is known as the Interpol National Central Bureau (NCB) for that country. In England the NCB is Scotland Yard; in France it is the Sureté (somewhat equivalent to the FBI in the United States). The NCB for

A Uniformed Division officer guards the entrance to the White House. Agents are responsible for protecting the president's home.

the United States—Interpol USA—is the Treasury Department, and specifically the Treasury's law-enforcement division, the Secret Service. Twenty-four hours a day, Interpol USA relays information to and from Interpol for all agencies of our government in an effort to cope with crime and criminals crossing our borders.

Protecting important political figures and securing the money supply of our country are difficult assignments. The organizational structure of the Secret Service is designed to meet these objectives in an effective and efficient manner.

A Secret Service agent signals to the press that they may not come any closer to President Carter.

FIVE

Becoming an Agent

Every year, the Secret Service hires individuals to help combat counterfeiting and protect the president. Sometimes, the agency actively recruits employees to fill highly specialized jobs within the organization. For example, if the Secret Service needs handwriting or fingerprint experts, the agency will contact other government agencies in search of qualified personnel. The Secret Service may also turn to local or state law-enforcement agencies for specially trained individuals.

Colleges also provide a source of new employees. Because criminal methods are becoming more sophisticated, the Secret Service will often employ college graduates with advanced skills in computer technology, accounting, electrical engineering, and research psychology.

However, the most sought after position within the Secret Service is that of special agent, and the selection and training process for this position is extremely rigorous. The Secret Service hires as special agents only those people who display exceptional intelligence, commitment, physical conditioning, integrity, and other characteristics vital to assuring the protection of the president and U.S. currency. In fact, the Secret Service accepts only 1 recruit from every 700 applications it receives. The low acceptance rate is due to the agency's high standards and low attrition rate. Once individuals join the agency, most stay for 20 years or longer. Women have been hired by the Secret Service as law-enforcement agents since December 26, 1971. Female agents have the same physical requirements as male agents whether or not the agent is a counterfeit expert or in the Presidential Protective Division. The number of female agents in the Secret Service has grown from 5, hired in 1971, to around 150 today.

The process of becoming a special agent begins when an individual fills out a federal employment application (SF-171), which can be obtained at the nearest U.S. Post Office, U.S. Office of Personnel Management regional branch, or Secret Service Field Office. The application asks questions regarding education, experience, past criminal record, age, sex, and physical qualifications.

Secret Service recruits are sworn in by the assistant secretary of the Treasury in 1971. Applicants must pass a rigorous selection and training process.

Secret Service agents (foreground) link hands to keep the crowd away from President and Mrs. Lyndon B. Johnson as they stroll near the White House.

Once the application is submitted, it is reviewed by Secret Service employees who make sure the applicant meets the agency's basic employment requirements. To advance in the selection process, applicants must be at least 21 years old and be less than 35 years old and have a bachelor's degree; a minimum of 3 years' employment experience of which at least 2 are in criminal investigation; or a comparable combination of experience and education. College-level study in any field is acceptable. The applicant must also display excellent physical condition, with weight in proportion to height and 20/40 vision in each eye, correctable to 20/20.

An applicant who meets these requirements is interviewed by Secret Service employees to determine his or her level of interest and appropriateness for the job. At this initial interview, applicants may be asked why they want to enter law enforcement; why they want to join the Secret Service in particular; and whether they understand the dangers inherent in the job.

If these questions are answered satisfactorily, applicants then take a series of written tests designed to determine their intelligence. An applicant who

Counterfeit or Genuine?

Since 1865 the Secret Service has trained agents to recognize the differences between genuine and counterfeit money. Even without such intensive training, however, the average person can also learn to detect counterfeit bills. The easiest way to determine whether a questionable bill is counterfeit is to compare it closely to another bill of the same denomination known to be genuine. The quality of the paper and the engraving should be the same.

What are the characteristics of genuine paper money? Genuine money is printed from engraved steel plates by experts at the Bureau of Engraving and Printing (another division of the Treasury Department). Unlike many foreign currencies, American money is printed on paper that does not contain watermarks (designs that are placed in the mold when paper is processed and that become visible when the paper is held up to the light). Instead, the paper is embedded with tiny red and blue silk fibers. Counterfeit paper currency does not contain these fibers, although counterfeiters have attempted to simulate them on the surface of their paper by printing red and blue lines.

Counterfeit paper money is usually printed using the photo-offset process. In this process, the negative from a photograph of a genuine bill is used to etch the design of the bill onto a flexible metal plate. The plate is curved to fit a revolving cylinder on a printing press and then the design of the bill is transferred to, or offset on, the paper by using a rubber blanket that runs over another cylinder. The image produced by offset printing is usually flat, dark, and blurry. Genuine currency, on the other hand, has a sharp design and all of the engraved lines are distinct. Areas on the bill where such differences are particularly evident are the Treasury Seal, the borders of the bill, and the serial number. On genuine bills, these are

Important features on a genuine $20 bill.

clear, evenly spaced, and unbroken.

Some counterfeit bills, particularly those produced by amateurs, contain the wrong portrait or back design. On the genuine $1 bill, George Washington and the Great Seal of the United States appear. Abraham Lincoln and the Lincoln Memorial are printed on the $5 bill; Alexander Hamilton and the U.S. Treasury Building are on the $10 bill; Andrew Jackson and the White House are on the $20 bill; Ulysses S. Grant and the U.S. Capitol are on the $50 bill; and Benjamin Franklin and Independence Hall are on the $100 bill.

The Secret Service informs banks of counterfeit bills known to be in circulation through a service called the Counterfeit Note Index. A description of each new counterfeit bill circulated is mailed to every bank in the U.S. The Secret Service's field offices also keep mailing lists of businesspeople to whom they send warnings about counterfeit bills appearing in their areas.

Another type of counterfeiting with which the Secret Service must deal involves genuine paper money that has been altered to increase its face value. A common method is to paste numerals from a higher denomination in the corners of a note of lower denomination. These counterfeit bills, called raised notes, are easily detected by comparing the portrait with the back design and the numerals—if they do not correspond, the bill is counterfeit.

Counterfeit coins are not as common as counterfeit bills. Usually they are copies of rare coins. Unlike genuine coins, which are produced by a

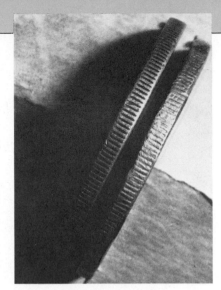

A genuine coin (left) and a counterfeit coin (right).

stamping machine, most counterfeit coins are manufactured by pouring molten metal into molds or dies. Coins made in the latter manner are often marked by irregularities, such as die stains, cracks, and metal blemishes. Some counterfeiters simulate rare coins by altering the date or mint mark (the tiny initial that identifies the location of production, such as *D* for Denver) of unexceptional genuine coins. Counterfeit coins can most easily be recognized by checking the corrugated outer edges, also known as reeding. On genuine coins the reeding is regular and readily apparent, but on counterfeit coins it may be uneven, crooked, or nonexistent.

Counterfeiting U.S. currency or altering it to increase its value is a violation of federal law and is punishable by a fine of up to $5,000, 15 years' imprisonment, or both, depending on the type of crime, amount of money involved, and the history of the offender.

An agent escorts Amy Carter, daughter of the president, to school in 1977. Agents must also protect members of the immediate families of the president and vice-president.

passes these tests is next given a panel interview designed to measure his or her ability to communicate. This interview is conducted by a group of special agents who ask a wide range of questions in an effort to decide whether the applicant can handle the job. For example, an agent must be willing to accept the routine of the job—some work assignments will take agents out of town at a moment's notice.

After completion of the panel interview, a small number of successful applicants are asked to continue in the selection process by filling out an information sheet, which asks a variety of questions regarding the applicant's personal and professional background: What are the applicant's work habits? Does the applicant have a good sense of humor? Will the applicant's family be able to cope with the routine? To help ensure the validity of the information provided by the applicant, a lie-detector test is administered.

Applicants must also pass a comprehensive medical examination to assure good physical condition. Every applicant's background and record is investigated with great thoroughness.

Stand-ins wearing placards rehearse the inauguration of President-elect Carter. Teamwork and planned strategy decrease the possible dangers to the president and his entourage.

The names of applicants who pass all these requirements are placed on the Secret Service job roster, and they are notified and offered assignments when positions open at the agency.

Training for new special agents is also rigorous. Two weeks after reporting to their field office assignments, special agents travel to the Federal Law Enforcement Training Center in Glynco, Georgia, where they study general law-enforcement principles. Here, for two months, new agents learn how to arrest suspected criminals, how to conduct legal search and seizure, and the laws of arrest. Agents also study police-community relations, basic theories of criminal behavior, criminal law, self-defense, use of deadly force, and first aid.

A short time after completing this basic training in Georgia, agents are sent to Secret Service training facilities located in the Washington, D.C., area. Here, agents learn the skills specific to their careers as special agents. New agents are given extensive training in counterfeit detection and fraud and forgery identification. They learn to recognize the slight inconsistencies that distinguish genuine currency from counterfeit money. Agents study the special paper and ink the Treasury Department uses; they are shown hundreds of counterfeit bills and certificates and are taught to determine their flaws. Agents are also trained to investigate credit card counterfeiting and fraud. They are able to recognize counterfeit cards by comparing ink colors, embossing, and the plastic composition of the fake cards. By the time agents complete their initial training, they are qualified counterfeit experts able to tell at a glance if currency or credit cards are genuine or counterfeit.

But counterfeit detection is only part of the training. Agents also learn the skills vital to protecting the president and others. They study how to conduct identification checks, set up barricades, control crowds, shield the person they are protecting from gunfire, and coordinate a motorcade. Agents are taught where to stand in relation to the person being protected and how to escort him or her in any number of circumstances.

New agents also receive instruction about the importance of teamwork. Each agent learns a number of different roles and if the president were ever harmed, he or she could instantly do any one of the many things required: radio the hospital, subdue the assailant, drive the president quickly to the hospital, control the public at the scene, or any additional action. During training, agents are thoroughly briefed on the vital tasks they might need to perform. They are made exceedingly aware of the possible dangers they will face, as well as how to decrease the chances of being harmed.

The job of a Secret Service agent is among the most important and demanding in all of government. Protecting the president from injury and safeguarding the U.S. money supply from counterfeiting often exposes agents to great personal danger. To increase their safety and the safety of those they protect, the Secret Service accepts only the best applicants into its ranks and then provides these individuals with the training necessary to perform their jobs successfully.

President Johnson shakes hands as his limousine passes a crowd. An agent walks beside the car to protect the president.

SIX

Protecting the President: Problems and Procedures

The Secret Service must contend with two constant demands. On the one hand, the American people expect to see their president frequently. They want him to make public appearances and personally address their many concerns. On the other hand, Americans desire total protection of their president. No security measure seems too extreme if it results in the safety of the country's top leader.

In many ways, these demands are incompatible. Every time the president appears publicly, he risks an assassination attempt. There is no way to protect him, at least not totally. Angry and mentally disturbed people can plot elaborate crimes, including kidnapping and murder. They can conceal guns and other weapons. For every security measure the Secret Service develops, a resourceful mind can construct a counterstrategy devised to harm the president.

The only way to fully protect our highest government officials is to lock them away from the public, behind bulletproof windows and locked doors. But that is not how the American people want their officials treated. That is also not how the president and vice-president have traditionally wished to be seen. They want to display an interest in meeting the people and observing the country firsthand.

In San Francisco, California, Secret Service agents hastily grab President Ford after he was shot at by a severely disturbed woman, Sara Moore.

Jimmy Carter, who was elected president in 1976, disliked much of the pomp and ceremony that surrounded the presidency. He replaced the armor-plated limousines that former presidents had used with smaller, less conspicuous automobiles. He also made frequent public appearances, often on a moment's notice without giving the Secret Service enough time to make proper security arrangements.

At his inaugural parade in 1976, Carter and his wife, Rosalynn, left their well-protected car and walked down Pennsylvania Avenue in Washington, D.C. Carter hoped the gesture would symbolize a president who was close to his people. However, by leaving his bulletproof automobile, the president exposed himself to great physical danger. The streets were lined with people. Anyone carrying a handgun could have shot President Carter and his wife, with the Secret Service helpless to stop it. But the well-trained agents quickly adapted to the situation. They surrounded the couple as closely as possible and walked with them to the White House.

Such are the circumstances the Secret Service often faces in guarding the president and other important officials. They must provide protection that does not unduly isolate the president from the people. To accomplish this, the agency has developed highly intricate techniques that protect government officials without disrupting the important work they do.

In 1977, President Carter and his wife, Rosalynn, wave to the crowds as they break tradition by walking the entire length of the inaugural parade route from the Capitol to the White House. Alarmed by the couple's vulnerability, Secret Service agents walked beside them serving as shields.

When the president resides at the White House the Secret Service follows a daily schedule of security checks that are known to few people, including the president. Secret Service agents examine the president's food to make sure it has not been tampered with or poisoned. The president's food is obtained only from selected suppliers and is transported to the White House in secure vehicles. There, it is prepared by trusted chefs, who have been cleared by security. Other kitchen workers are investigated thoroughly before they are employed and are constantly monitored while at the White House.

Secret Service precautions are equally stringent in the White House mail room. Each day, the president receives hundreds of thousands of cards and letters. Many are written by concerned citizens who wish to express opinions on a variety of issues. Other letters come from children as part of school assignments. White House staff members read much of the mail; the president sees little of it because of his heavy schedule. But the mail that the president does see is first carefully scrutinized by the Secret Service. If a piece of mail appears suspicious, the package or letter is analyzed by explosives experts.

Secret Service agents are equally concerned about unseen dangers—particularly the threat of radiation contamination. To prevent an assassin from poisoning the president with radiation, Secret Service agents regularly monitor the White House with sensitive instruments that detect the presence of radioactive contaminants. On a daily basis, agents also conduct simpler radiation tests that involve exposing radiation-sensitive film in key White House rooms.

But the bulk of the president's protection comes from the Secret Service's constant physical surveillance. Whether the president is working, sleeping, eating, or relaxing, agents stand silent watch, making sure no one harms him.

At the White House, the protection begins on the front lawn, where the personnel of the Uniformed Division keep the public away from the building's large front entrance. Officers use hidden cameras to scan the crowds. They look for suspicious individuals and intercept intruders who may try to climb over the White House fence.

Closer to the building, special agents discourage attacks against the president's home or office by patrolling the area. Inside, members of the Presidential Protective Division are stationed in such a way as to provide the president with the maximum amount of security.

Members of the Presidential Protective Division include some of the most competent law-enforcement officers in the world. The officers are trained observers who can identify suspicious individuals before they can do harm.

To ensure the president's safety, an agent searches under a draped table in a hotel ballroom before President Ford addresses a dinner audience.

They also know a variety of self-defense disciplines, including karate and boxing.

When the president travels, he receives similar protection. Security for a presidential trip begins weeks, sometimes months before the president sets out for his destination. The long preparation is imperative, because outside the White House the Secret Service faces a great many variables that could pose risks to the president's safety.

Consequently, security plans begin when a Secret Service advance team journeys to the city the president expects to visit. This team consists of agents from the Presidential Protective Division and the Office of Protective Research. These agents work with members of the president's personal staff, local police, and city officials. Together, these professionals develop a security plan to ensure the safety of the president while in a particular city.

71

Based on the security plan, the advance team devises a timetable for the president's visit. At each stop, they consider what risks the president may face and implement plans to minimize these dangers. For example, the advance team will visit the hotel or other building where the president plans to stay. There, they map the building's layout, considering places where an assassin could hide. Agents also check the elevators, making sure they are safe. They inspect the kitchen to determine how best to monitor its workers while the president's meals are prepared.

After each location on the president's schedule is inspected, the advance team broadens its investigation to include the surrounding area. With help from

A presidential motorcade is led by a police pilot car and followed by motorcycle police who survey the crowds along the route.

The presidential jetliner, Air Force One, also called the Flying White House, is a Boeing 707 and can fly more than 7,000 miles nonstop. Agents protect the president during all of his flights.

the Office of Protective Research, the Secret Service determines the names of people in the vicinity who might be a threat. Agents then visit these people. If an individual is determined to be a threat, the Secret Service may designate an agent or a local policeman to keep the person under surveillance. As the last step, the Secret Service distributes to agents and police photographs or descriptions of dangerous individuals who should not be allowed near the president.

Finally, the advance team holds a pre-visit briefing that establishes specific responsibilities for agents, local police, and other law-enforcement officers on hand to protect the president. During a presidential motorcade, a systematic procedure is also followed. The motorcade is led by police vehicles, and police survey the area for potential problems. A police pilot car follows next to inform law-enforcement officers along the route that the president is actually on the way. Another squad of police vehicles is followed by an unmarked police car that carries high-ranking local police officials and Secret Service officials.

The next car in the motorcade is the presidential limousine. In the rear sit the president and accompanying guests. Police vehicles are positioned in such a way as to keep the public from approaching the car.

Directly behind the president's limousine, a specially designed Secret Service car carries agents, who scan the crowd searching for possible problems. They are trained to spot quick movements that could be the tipoff of an assassination attempt.

Behind the Secret Service are an assortment of police vehicles, cars with photographers and reporters, and communications vehicles that carry audio and video links with news agencies around the world.

To cover greater distances, the president travels in Air Force One, a large passenger-jet aircraft specially designed for security. Guarded by the Air Force 24 hours a day to prevent sabotage, the jet is outfitted with office and sleeping space for the president, members of his staff, the press, and the Secret Service.

Special precautions are taken to assure the safety of the president while aboard Air Force One. One precaution is to keep all other aircraft out of the vicinity of the presidential plane. When taxiing on the runway, Air Force One is followed by fire trucks and an ambulance.

For the men and women who must protect the president, the job entails tremendous pressure and many long and difficult hours. Members of the Secret Service are sworn to sacrifice their lives, if necessary, to save the life of the president. They are ready at a moment's notice to take life-threatening action to thwart an assassination or kidnapping attempt. Psychiatrists claim that the stress Secret Service agents face while guarding the president is similar to that experienced by jet fighter pilots. They must always be prepared and have no room for error. Even a second's delay could result in injury or harm to the president. It is a nerve-racking job that calls for commitment and dedication. An agent on a protective detail must be bodyguard, detective, chaperone, tour guide, police officer, and weapons expert.

Although many of these jobs sound exciting, there is another side to protecting the president that is much less interesting. Because agents must constantly watch the president, much time is spent standing alone in deserted hallways waiting for the president to finish a meeting or sleep through the night. Called "post standers," the agents are not allowed to socialize or become distracted. They must remain on their feet, guarding against every possible intrusion.

Agents take turns standing post. Shifts are rotated every two weeks, so the same agents do not have the night shift continuously. Although the shifts usually pass quietly, events do occur that show the need for constant surveillance. An interesting example occurred during one of President Richard Nixon's brief vacations at his home in San Clemente, California.

Upon arriving at San Clemente, the president retired to his study. Although the weather was warm, Nixon asked an assistant to start a fire in the fireplace. This was a common practice for Nixon, who enjoyed working next to a warm fire and often turned on the air conditioner to avoid overheating the house.

Outside Nixon's home the Secret Service kept a careful evening watch over the president.

Once the fire started burning, a smoke alarm began to buzz in the Secret Service command post a quarter-mile away. The agents on duty thought

A female agent (foreground) guards the limousine carrying President Carter. The Secret Service first hired women as law-enforcement agents in 1971.

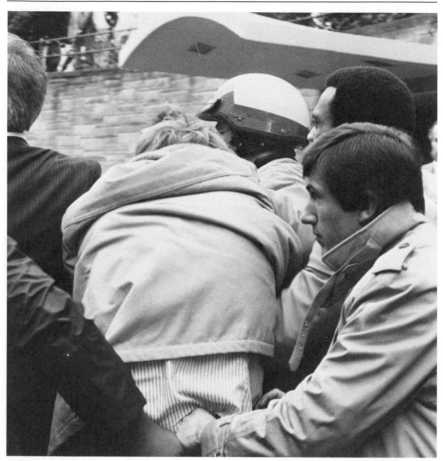

Policemen and Secret Service agents seize John M. Hinckley after he shot President Reagan in 1981. Although Hinckley fired six shots into the crowd, the agents' swift action after hearing the first shot prevented Hinckley from killing the president.

nothing of the incident, believing that smoke from the fireplace had tripped the alarm. Soon, however, a smoke detector in another part of the house again triggered the alarm. A visual inspection revealed that a strange fog had settled around the house.

The Secret Service became concerned and telephoned a servant inside the house to ask him to see if anything was wrong. By this time President Nixon had gone to bed. The servant quickly returned to the telephone, shouting, "Call the fire department! Call the fire department! The house is full of smoke!"

At that moment, the Secret Service did not know the severity of the blaze or whether it posed a threat to the president. But one agent immediately called the San Clemente Fire Department while another radioed the agent standing guard outside Nixon's bedroom and told him to move the president to safety outside the house.

The Secret Service approached the house and entered it. The first floor was completely filled with smoke. Agents dragged a fire hose into the president's study, where the smoke was thickest. They soon realized that heat from the fireplace had overheated two steel rods that supported its brick and mortar, and that the rods had ignited the surrounding wall. Agents doused the flame with water until it was extinguished.

By the time the fire department arrived, everything was under control and the fire was out. Afterward, an investigation showed that the fire was more serious than originally imagined. Because the inside of the walls was burning, the house could have been destroyed if the Secret Service agents had not acted quickly.

Although agents who protect the president are courageous men and women, they must daily face the possibility of mortal danger. At any given time, the president's life could be threatened by an assassin or a kidnapper. In the process, an agent could be shot or killed. Secret Service agents must consciously work to suppress the fear of being injured. They must also fight the fear of not responding appropriately under pressure. Because attempts against the president's life are rare, agents often question whether they will react with the proper force and speed if events call for swift action.

Secret Service agents protect President Reagan's limousine during a visit to the president's hometown, Dixon, Illinois.

SEVEN

The Secret Service: Today and Tomorrow

For more than 100 years, the Secret Service has built a reputation of excellence in law enforcement. Established in 1865, the agency's original responsibility was to combat the widespread counterfeiting of U.S. currency. But its responsibilities were steadily increased during the late 1880s to include criminal investigation. After the assassination of President William McKinley in 1901, the Secret Service gained its most important duty—the protection of the president of the United States.

The Secret Service has worked to improve its ability to carry out its responsibilities. The agency's commitment to innovative protection strategies and techniques has kept it one step ahead of many dangerous criminals.

But no system or procedure is foolproof. As long as the president and other government officials make public appearances, their lives will be at risk. The assassination of President Kennedy in 1963 is a reminder of that fact. The Secret Service functions under difficult and imperfect conditions. It offers protection to officials who must be available to the public. Although the investigation into Kennedy's assassination cleared the Secret Service of any blame, this tragedy led the agency to correct some important shortfalls. Perhaps as a consequence, not a single government official under Secret Service protection has been killed since Kennedy's assassination.

The Secret Service's protective duties have grown substantially since 1901. Today, agents guard the president, the vice-president, the president-elect, and vice-president-elect. The Secret Service also protects the first family, the vice-president's family, former presidents, their unmarried widows, and their children until the age of 16. Agents safeguard distinguished foreign visitors and major presidential candidates and their spouses.

Protecting all these individuals is a difficult and challenging assignment that the Secret Service accomplishes with 4,300 employees throughout the United States. Many of these employees are stationed at one of the Secret Service's 63 field offices or 49 resident agent offices. In the field, agents provide regional protection to visiting officials but spend the majority of their time investigating

A month after an explosion caused by terrorists killed 237 U.S. Marines in Beirut, Lebanon, in October 1983, trucks were placed at the front gates of the White House to barricade it against attack. In addition to a Uniformed Division officer who patrols the scene, concrete barriers now secure the roadblock.

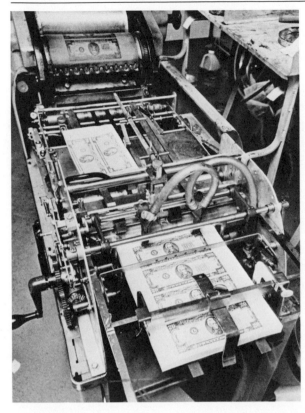

An offset printing press with counterfeit $20 bills still in place. The equipment and counterfeit money were seized by the Secret Service during a raid in 1977.

counterfeiting and forgery cases. To perform these roles, Secret Service agents work closely with local police and federal law-enforcement agencies, such as the FBI.

To apprehend counterfeiters, the Secret Service follows tips that come from various sources. In fact, the Secret Service asks people who suspect they possess counterfeit bills or coins to contact the agency immediately. The telephone number is usually printed on the inside cover of every telephone book or listed under Federal Government Agencies or Law Enforcement Agencies. It is also listed in the blue pages devoted to city, state, and federal government numbers at the rear of many metropolitan telephone books.

Once the Secret Service receives a reliable tip about a counterfeiter, it employs a variety of investigative techniques, including fingerprints, lie-detector tests, informants, manhunts, and stakeouts to catch the offender. The agency's record of success is impressive. In 1986, for instance, the Secret Service closed 129 counterfeiting plants and confiscated nearly $46 million worth of counterfeit notes and coins. Along the way, agents arrested 1,682 people for counterfeiting, 4,679 people for forging government checks, and 54 people for counterfeiting government bonds.

The future holds even greater challenges for the Secret Service. In protecting government officials, the agency is investigating new computer technologies that can help agents identify and keep records on people who may pose a threat to the president. The Secret Service is also evaluating new, highly effective weapons that agents can use to discourage potential assassins or kidnappers. To shield the president and other officials, technicians in the Secret Service's Office of Protective Research are analyzing new, super-strong plastics that are lighter than steel but offer more protection. Installed in the presidential limousine, these plastics may provide increased protection from bullets.

One new concern for the Secret Service is the increased threat of terrorism, or violence committed in support of a particular political goal or ideology. Terrorism is difficult to stop because those who take part in the violence often care little about their own safety. Consequently, a terrorist may drive a truck loaded with explosives to its target and detonate it, killing him- or herself and everyone else in the area.

Another terrorist tactic that Secret Service agents must guard against is kidnapping. A terrorist could kidnap a member of the first family for ransom money or perhaps to make political demands.

The Secret Service has undertaken a number of precautions to prevent terrorist acts from being committed against the president and other important officials. Because of national security implications, most protective measures are classified as top secret. Still, the Secret Service discloses that it works closely with other agencies to identify terrorist groups.

Similar challenges confront the Secret Service in combating counterfeiting. Recent technological advances in the printing industry have put copying ability well in the reach of many Americans. Along with experts in other sections of the Treasury Department, the Secret Service is evaluating printing technologies that would make the detection of counterfeiting a relatively simple process. One method prints a hologram, or laser-generated image, of the United States seal on paper money; this hologram looks three-dimensional under ordinary light. Such innovations must be thoroughly evaluated and, if adopted, introduced carefully, because the government is concerned that a sudden major change might undermine confidence in U.S. currency throughout the world.

President Reagan; his wife, Nancy; and Secret Service agents leave the hospital after the president's recuperation from wounds received in the Hinckley assassination attempt.

Despite sophisticated new technologies, the government will continue to rely on the men and women of the U.S. Secret Service to combat fraud, forgery, and counterfeiting. The same holds true for protecting the president and other officials. No matter how complex electronic or automatic systems may be, criminals will try to devise schemes for getting around them. No technology is as effective as a dedicated Secret Service agent, who can function in a great variety of situations. No computer can replace the careful watch of an agent's well-trained eye and his or her ability to evaluate the meaning of what is seen and make a quick decision about what action to take. The job of safeguarding the president rests with people who pledge their lives to protect the nation's highest official.

The job of a Secret Service agent is often a stressful, anonymous position. An agent's career can end with an assassin's bullet or a terrorist's bomb. But for the employees of the Secret Service, protecting the president can also be an immensely rewarding challenge.

United States Secret Service

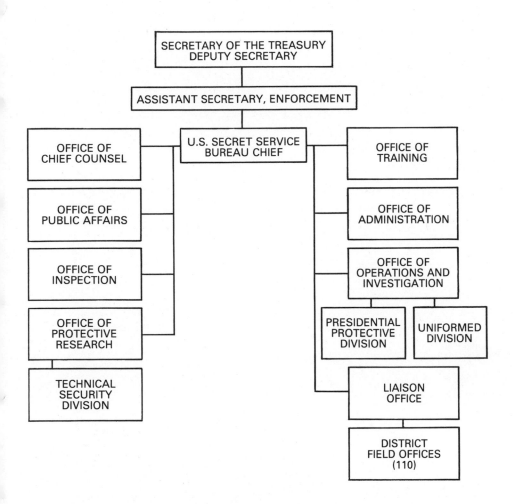

SECRETARY OF THE TREASURY
DEPUTY SECRETARY

ASSISTANT SECRETARY, ENFORCEMENT

U.S. SECRET SERVICE
BUREAU CHIEF

OFFICE OF
CHIEF COUNSEL

OFFICE OF
PUBLIC AFFAIRS

OFFICE OF
INSPECTION

OFFICE OF
PROTECTIVE
RESEARCH

TECHNICAL
SECURITY
DIVISION

OFFICE OF
TRAINING

OFFICE OF
ADMINISTRATION

OFFICE OF
OPERATIONS AND
INVESTIGATION

PRESIDENTIAL
PROTECTIVE
DIVISION

UNIFORMED
DIVISION

LIAISON
OFFICE

DISTRICT
FIELD OFFICES
(110)

GLOSSARY

Assassinate To murder a prominent person, usually violently.

Counterfeit The illegal production of imitation coins, bills, credit cards, or other securities with a monetary value.

Currency Coins, government notes, and bank notes in circulation as a medium of exchange.

Field offices The Secret Service operational centers that are located throughout the country and are responsible for activities in specific geographic areas.

Forgery The crime of deliberately altering a document.

Fraud An intentional misrepresentation in order to gain property or legal rights.

Interpol The acronym for the International Criminal Police Organization, an agency that works to apprehend criminals who cross national borders.

Mint To produce coins under the authority of a government.

Sniper A person who fires a weapon at an exposed person.

Terrorism The systematic use of violence as a means of political coercion.

SELECTED REFERENCES

Baughman, U. E., and L. Robinson. *Secret Service Chief.* New York: Harper & Row, 1962.

Clarke, James W. *American Assassins: The Darker Side of Politics.* Princeton, NJ: Princeton University Press, 1982.

Colby, C. B. *Secret Service History, Duties, and Equipment.* New York: Coward-McCann, 1966.

Dorman, Michael. *The Secret Service Story.* New York: Delacorte Press, 1967.

Epstein, Edward J. *Inquest: The Warren Commission and the Establishment of Truth.* New York: Viking Press, 1966.

Jeffreys-Jones, Rhodri. *American Espionage: From Secret Service to CIA.* New York: Free Press, 1977.

Know Your Money. Washington: U.S. Government Printing Office, 1985.

Landress, M. M. *I Made It Myself.* New York: Random House, 1965.

McCarthy, Dennis, and Philip Smith. *Protecting the President.* New York: Dell, 1985.

McKinley, James. *Assassination in America.* New York: Harper & Row, 1977.

Motto, Carmine J. *Undercover.* Springfield, IL: Thomas, 1971.

Neal, Harry E. *Secret Service in Action.* New York: Lodestar Books, 1980.

Wilson, Frank J., and Beth Day. *Special Agent.* New York: Gregg Publishing Co., 1932.

Youngblood, Rufus W. *20 Years in the Secret Service: My Life With Five Presidents.* New York: Simon & Schuster, 1973.

INDEX

Gregory Matusky graduated from the University of Pennsylvania. He holds degrees in communications, English, and marketing, and, with John P. Hayes, wrote *King Hussein* for the WORLD LEADERS— PAST & PRESENT series published by Chelsea House.

John P. Hayes teaches journalism at Temple University in Philadelphia. He is the author of *James A. Michener: A Biography* and several other books and many articles. Dr. Hayes, his wife, and their three children reside in North Hills, Pennsylvania.

Arthur M. Schlesinger, jr., served in the White House as special assistant to Presidents Kennedy and Johnson. He is the author of numerous acclaimed works in American history and has twice been awarded the Pulitzer Prize. He taught history at Harvard College for many years and is currently Albert Schweitzer Professor of the Humanities at the City College of New York.